To:

....

From:

....

FIND REST

A women's devotional
for lasting peace

SHAUNTI
FELDHAHN

Foreword

Overcommitted and overwhelmed.
Hurried and harried.
Racing at warp speed and running on empty.
Out of breath and on edge.
Can't keep up and can't slow down.
Expended and exhausted.
Wrung out and worn out.
Depleted and defeated.
Stretched and stressed.
Anxious and restless.

Sound familiar?

This is what I often sense when I look into the eyes and hearts of my Christian sisters.

All too often, it's what I see when I slow down long enough to consider what's going on in my own soul.

And based on what Shaunti has written in these twenty short devotional readings, I'd say she's no stranger to this same breathless-on-the-treadmill-of-life sort of experience.

Yet she understands, and she wants us to understand, that the gospel (and this is Good News indeed) calls us to another way.

God's Word promises us green pastures and still waters, times of refreshing rivers of living water flowing from within.

So from one needy pilgrim to another, I invite you to push pause, step into these pages, let your mind be renewed, and let your racing heart slow down.

Mostly I invite you come to Christ. And in Him, find:

Grace and gratitude.
Contentment and courage.
Peace and perspective.
Dependence and delight.
Trust and thriving.
Strength and sanity.
A slower pulse and steady praise.
Worship and wonder.
Restoration and refreshing.
In a word, rest.

Our Savior beckons to you and to me:
"Stand by the roads, and look,
and ask for the ancient paths,
where the good way is; and walk in it,
and find rest for your souls."
— Jeremiah 6:16

Stop your running, He says. Stand still. Look at the way you're heading. Ask for directions to a new and different place (actually an ancient place). Walk in that good way— His way, the paths walked by those who have gone before us. Find rest for your soul.

— Nancy DeMoss Wolgemuth

A Personal Note

Dear Friends,

Life is so busy, isn't it? We are constantly rushing from here to there. Whether it's with kids, work, volunteering, school, marriage or dating, meetings, soccer games, friendships—the list goes *on*! We often feel pulled and stretched beyond our capacity, only to find the craziness starting all over the next morning when the alarm clock rings.

What's a woman to do in such a whirlwind life?

People tell us that all we need to do is just . . . slow down. Take a break. Relax. But let's be honest, ladies. That may be great advice for a short time but it is usually not realistic for a lifetime. As much as we enjoy days off to unwind, that isn't *everyday* life—there's just a lot to do! And so much God *wants* us to do!

Since I'm both a follower of Christ and a researcher, I've been studying what both the Bible and science says about this. And Jesus actually gives a startling solution in Matthew: "Take my yoke upon you. Let me teach you, because I am humble and gentle at heart, and you will find rest for your souls." (Matthew 11:29 NLT).

A yoke fits an animal so it can do the good work of the day without stress. Jesus *doesn't* say to set aside the yoke and head back to the barn to find rest. Instead, he says that by working under His guidance in our everyday lives, we can still be busy—but we don't have to be stressed. We will find *rest for our souls.*

Sisters, so much of the stress and worry we face each day doesn't have to be there! Often, we are missing a few key truths about our mind-set, actions, or level of trust in a God whose mercies are new every morning. I've compiled a list of eight elements to finding rest that both science and scripture says we need to consider. (See the Elements of Finding Rest on page vi.) With each devotional day, we will take a step toward being the kind of woman who lives a life marked by the rest Jesus promises.

One final note: this is a small book based on the main devotional called Find Rest: A Women's Devotional for Lasting Peace in a Busy Life. If you are blessed by this sample, please consider continuing the full journey to find true rest for your soul!

— Shaunti Feldhahn

Elements of Finding Rest

- Build Only on Rock
- Live According to Your Design
- Set Aside Superwoman
- Connect with God
- Shift Your Perspective
- Create Life-Giving Relationships
- Walk in Obedience
- Have No Fear

Thus says the LORD: "Stand by the roads, and
look, and ask for the ancient paths, where the good
way is; and walk in it, and find rest for your souls."
— Jeremiah 6:16, ESV

Finding Your Good Way

When I moved to New York City in 1994, I spent a lot of time on the subway. Always busy, I enjoyed speeding under the gridlocked traffic to quickly reach my destination. Most of Manhattan is laid out in a clear grid pattern with numbered streets, so getting around is easy.

As long as you know where you are, you know exactly where to go. I'm at 32nd and Park, so I just need to head north two blocks and turn right on 34th street.

There is just one hitch: When you come off the subway at an unfamiliar stop, how do you know where you are? Surrounded by tall buildings, you have no sense of direction.

In those days, there was an easy solution: we would turn in a circle until we spotted the Twin Towers, which were clearly visible at the southern tip of Manhattan. We knew that was south, so we could use that landmark to determine where we were and where to go. We based our sense of direction on the Twin Towers because they were fixed and unmoving.

Until they weren't. On September 11, 2001, every New Yorker —and every person on the planet, really—saw the truth that all man-made things are temporary.

In our crazy, modern lives, each of us is looking for direction: how do we get to that life of peace and joy we want, rather than the stressed and frazzled life we have? All too often, we base our decisions on things that loom large in our eyes—convenience, the advice of friends, whether it avoids pain or brings pleasure. But those factors are a fickle guide.

We are stressed and frazzled because we have followed temporary directional signals that do not lead to peace (the "good way," as the prophet Jeremiah put it).

Jesus quoted the prophet Jeremiah when he said there is only one way to find that good way: taking on His yoke and learning from Him. (Matthew 11:29).

We must stop looking to temporary signals for a sense of direction. We must look to the One who both never changes and is gentle with our human, frazzled state. As we will see on Day 2, His yoke (guiding force) will never pull us astray.

Reflect

Think of a decision (small or large) that is causing you stress, that you need to make in the coming days. What temporary things might you be looking to for a sense of direction? (For example, the path of least resistance at the moment, or what your colleagues are suggesting you do...) What unchanging truth can you look to instead?

Notes

_____

_____

_____

_____

_____

_____

_____

_____

"WHEN I UNDERSTAND THAT EVERYTHING HAPPENING TO ME IS TO MAKE ME MORE CHRISTLIKE, IT RESOLVES A GREAT DEAL OF ANXIETY."

— A.W. Tozer

Come to me, all you who are weary and burdened,
and I will give you rest. Take my yoke upon you
and learn from me, for I am gentle and humble
in heart, and you will find rest for your souls.
— Matthew 11:28-29, NIV

His Yoke Is
Custom-Fit for You

When my children were small, money was very tight. The local annual consignment sales were a lifesaver for inexpensively outfitting two quickly-growing kids. I generally bought a size or two ahead so the kids had room to grow for the next year.

I thought the kids looked adorable in their oversized shirts and rolled-up jeans, but they were definitely not custom fit! I was asking them to live, play, and work in clothes that were not tailored to them in any way.

God is not like that. When Jesus says that a key way to find rest is to "Take my yoke upon you," He is gently rebuking us for taking on burdens that we were not meant to carry, and telling us to instead take on those purposes that He has created just for us.

A yoke is a device that hitches over the shoulders of a working animal (or team of animals) so they can comfortably pull something heavy, such as a plow. Since every animal is a different size and shape, a caring farmer carefully custom fits a yoke to each beast. This allows the ox or horse or donkey to work well when he is called upon, without getting exhausted, being ineffective from pulling at a wrong angle, or getting chafed and sore.

The farmer is also careful not to give a young animal a yoke that is too large. Instead, at every stage of growth, the farmer remeasures the beasts under his care and creates a new yoke. The animal is called to a particular purpose, and he is outfitted for it.

Imagine the difficulty if one animal were to take on the yoke that was designed for another. The ground might get plowed, but oh the pain and strain and heaviness! Oh, the open sores on a weary back! After days and months of this, wouldn't the animal eventually shy away from the good work of the day?

So often, we are weary and burdened not because of long hours or having too much to do, but because we are taking on things we were never meant to do, or in a way or during a time we were never meant to do them. Let us believe our Lord's promise that when we take up His yoke for us, we will find rest.

Reflect

What are you taking on that may not be God's
fit or design for you? How can you set that aside
and avoid that temptation in the future?

Notes

_____

_____

_____

_____

_____

_____

_____

_____

"SET YOURSELF EARNESTLY
TO SEE WHAT YOU ARE
MADE TO DO, AND THEN
SET YOURSELF EARNESTLY
TO DO IT."

— Phillips Brooks

It is useless for you to work so hard from early morning until late at night, anxiously working for food to eat; for God gives rest to his loved ones.
— *Psalm 127:2*

No More Superwoman!

Our society is tired. Dog tired. And women, specifically, seem to be the most tired of all. That's why we are tempted by the latest and greatest pill, potion, powder, or diet that will give us more energy.

Exhaustion has become the social norm amongst busy women. And let's admit the hard truth: We often find ourselves glorifying the busy schedules, giving ourselves a pat on the back when we squeeze one more commitment into an already too-packed day and admiring others who seem to handle the juggling act as if they were a professional in a three-ring circus.

Even crazier, we also tend to consider ourselves lazy if we want a break from our busy schedules. What am I doing sitting and reading a book for half an hour over lunch? I signed up to make party favors for the teacher appreciation event, and I have to turn in that report on the Boston merger tomorrow, and I need to clean the house before the dinner party tomorrow night!

As we push ourselves beyond what we were designed to bear, we also overlook the physical and emotional signs that we're doing too much. We rush at breakneck speed right into stress that God never intended us to bear. Remember? He gives rest to His loved ones.

There are basic elements of self-care—diet, exercise, and sleep—that will help create balance in our lives. We need to

do those things. But they don't solve the chronic problem. We have a bone-deep exhaustion because we are trying to be Superwoman. We have bought into the lie that we can have it all, do it all, and be it all—all at the same time.

We were not designed for that. We were designed to have to make choices. To prioritize. To realize that above a certain threshold, which is a whole lot lower than we like to think, every extra good thing we take on is a net negative for us and for God's purposes for our lives. We were not designed to be Superwomen. If we want to be in charge of teacher appreciation, that means being okay with warmly welcoming our guests the following night into a somewhat messy but loving home, populated by people who understand the art of putting their attention where it really matters.

Reflect

How might you be trying to have it all, all at the same time? How is that affecting you, and what is one thing you can do to change it?

Notes

_____

_____

_____

_____

_____

_____

_____

_____

"IF WE WANT TO LIVE A WHOLEHEARTED LIFE, WE HAVE TO BECOME INTENTIONAL ABOUT CULTIVATING SLEEP AND PLAY, AND ABOUT LETTING GO OF EXHAUSTION AS A STATUS SYMBOL AND PRODUCTIVITY AS SELF-WORTH."

— Brené Brown
The Gifts Of Imperfection

Do you not know? Have you not heard? The Lord is the everlasting God, the Creator of the ends of the earth. He will not grow tired or weary, and his understanding no one can fathom. He gives strength to the weary and increases the power of the weak.
— Isaiah 40:28-29, NIV

Plug into Your Source of Strength

We've all been there—our phone battery suddenly drops into the red zone just when an important call comes in. Will the battery hold out? Or will it go dead, leaving us sounding unprofessional? Or uncaring? Or simply unable to finish the important coordination with the home health aides who are checking on our elderly parents?

Finally we get to a place where we see a charger and outlet. We can breathe again as we continue the conversation, our battery power slowly creeping back up into the normal zone.

As women, our batteries often run dangerously low. We may try to plug into superficial power, such as an extra shot of espresso in the morning or some online shopping. Perhaps we rely on our friends to give us that boost to make us feel important and needed. Or we look to a boyfriend to fill the deep desire for love and affirmation.

But these power sources don't cut it. They can't quite get our battery to a full charge. We're left feeling frustrated, run down, let down, and even defeated.

There is only one real energy source, and it is not found at the

coffee shop. It is found in that moment when we come before the One who understands every minute detail about us and longs to give power to those who know they are weary and weak before Him.

You may feel like you need a nap, but He never grows weary. You may feel weak in the knees as you struggle to understand how to handle a difficult relationship, but He gives you strength. He provides guidance and wisdom and fills every single need of your heart. His charge will take hold and fill you. But here's the catch: You need to plug into Him.

Maybe that means adding time with God to your calendar every morning or joining a Bible study in order to read Scripture in a fresh way. Maybe it means listening to a sermon podcast while you make dinner or reaching out to a friend as an accountability partner who will remind you of the only true source of strength—God Himself.

Whatever method you try, it will make a dramatic difference in your life. God may not remove the circumstances that fill up your day, but He will give you the strength to walk with Him through it.

Reflect

In what way will you regularly plug
into God's power going forward?

Notes

_____

_____

_____

_____

_____

_____

_____

_____

"WE NEED TO FIND GOD, AND HE CANNOT BE FOUND IN NOISE AND RESTLESSNESS. GOD IS THE FRIEND OF SILENCE ... WE NEED SILENCE TO BE ABLE TO TOUCH SOULS."

— Mother Teresa

Whatever is true, whatever is noble, whatever is right, whatever is pure, whatever is lovely, whatever is admirable—if anything is excellent or praiseworthy—think about such things.
— *Philippians 4:8, NIV*

What You Focus on Is What You'll See

In the classic "Invisible Gorilla" experiment video, created by Harvard University in 1999, six people in black and white shirts pass basketballs back and forth. A voice asks the viewer to count how many times the people in white shirts pass the basketball.

Simple, right?

Half of those who watch the video miss something very, very obvious—a gorilla. Yes, someone in a gorilla suit actually walks through the basketball passers, very clearly faces the camera and thumps his chest, and then walks offscreen. Half of us are so busy counting the passes between the white-shirted people that we never even notice it. When the video asks, "Did you see the gorilla?" we think, *Wait, what gorilla?!*

What we focus on will change what we observe around us. We will notice more and more of what we focus on or, conversely, less and less of what we don't want to see.

In the research for my book *The Kindness Challenge*, I found that this is one of the main reasons for the unneeded stress in our lives, and one of the God-given ways to overcome it. As we focus on the things that annoy or anger us, well, you guessed it, we often completely miss some good and wonderful

stuff that could change how we feel. We miss the gorilla! So often, when we are worried about our struggling marriage, frustrations with an adult child, a roommate's messiness, or our mean coworker, that negative thing looms large in our eyes. We think about it, ponder it, express frustration about it. And we never even see the other spectacular things going on around us.

Yet, as we focus on "whatever is lovely"—those good and true things we like and appreciate—we'll find ourselves noticing those things more often. And as we do, our negative concerns won't loom as large.

Suppose that instead of asking why your husband loaded the dishwasher that way (again!), you give him a hug and thank him for cleaning up the kitchen. What will happen to your feelings? You'll feel better! And as you look for the next thing to praise . . . and the next . . . you'll find that you don't really even notice what annoyed you so much before. Instead, you'll start noticing everything you can be grateful for.

It's a shift in focus that God asks us to make because He knows it delivers a big impact.

Reflect

What three positive "gorillas" are you missing
because other worries are looming too large
in your eyes? How can you change that?

Notes

_____

_____

_____

_____

_____

_____

_____

_____

"NEVER LOSE AN OPPORTUNITY OF SEEING ANYTHING BEAUTIFUL, FOR BEAUTY IS GOD'S HANDWRITING."

— Ralph Waldo Emerson

Every day they continued to meet together in the temple courts. They broke bread in their homes and ate together with glad and sincere hearts, praising God and enjoying the favor of all the people.
— *Acts 2:46-47, NIV*

Created for Community

We were not created to do life alone. God looked at His creation and said "it is good," with one exception: it was absolutely not good for man to be alone. So God made someone with whom he could "do life." Then, in the first ever small group, God Himself walked in the garden with the man and his wife. Over and over in the Bible, God stresses that He designed us to love and support each other. We are directed (not asked) to live in community with other followers of Christ.

When I was living in Boston, a pastor shared a story about good friends who had moved to California. One night the pastor and his wife were awakened at 3 a.m. with an urgent phone call from their friends, asking for prayer. Raging wildfires were threatening their home and community. From their window, they could see the glow of thousands of acres burning, the fire advancing quickly as they raced to evacuate their home. The pastor and his wife got out of bed and knelt on the cold floor, praying urgently for an hour for the protection of their friends, their home, and everyone in the area.

In the end, although the fire consumed thousands of acres and several neighborhoods, the broader community—and their friends' house—was spared.

The homeowner called the pastor and thanked him profusely for being a true friend. The pastor answered, "No, thank you.

You were the one being a true friend. You thought enough of our friendship that you were willing to wake us up in the middle of the night to ask us to pray. You were good enough friends that you were willing to 'inconvenience' us."

Our lives can be consumed by wildfires—personal family struggles, having too much on our plates, difficulties managing our kids or careers, health concerns, and financial strains. We can see the fires on the horizon, advancing toward us, and our chest tightens as life comes at us so fast. But God has created community for us to call on—even in the middle of the night. Are you willing to inconvenience a fellow believer in order to live in authentic community? That is what God has designed for you. And your willingness to do so will be a blessing to you both.

Reflect

How could you be more engaged in Christian
community, including being willing to ask for
help? How might that help you find rest?

Notes

_____

_____

_____

_____

_____

_____

_____

_____

"CHRISTIANITY, SHARING THE CHRISTIAN FAITH IN COMMON, GIVES YOU INSTANT FRIENDSHIP, AND THAT IS THE REMARKABLE THING, BECAUSE IT TRANSCENDS CULTURE."

— John Lennox

So prepare your minds for action and exercise self-control.
Put all your hope in the gracious salvation that will come to
you when Jesus Christ is revealed to the world. So you must
live as God's obedient children. Don't slip back into your
old ways of living to satisfy your own desires.... You must be
holy in everything you do, just as God who chose you is holy.
— 1 Peter 1:13-15

Self-Control and Self-Consequences

If you are a parent, one of your greatest callings (and challenges!) is teaching your children self-control. "Yes, I know you wanted to hit your sister, but you have to stop yourself. You can't just hit someone because you feel like it." "Sure, your brother/friend/classmate tried to provoke you, but that doesn't mean you say mean things back. Make a good choice, honey." "Don't roll your eyes at me, young lady." (Okay, I had to add that one.)

A child experiences stress and heartache when they live to satisfy their own desires. Their friends won't play with them. They feel guilt for being mean. They are punished for their actions. In the end, they get hurt even more. This stress is the direct consequence for doing what God does not intend.

It's easy to see the consequences for failing to live God's way in our children, but sometimes we miss them in our own lives.

After college, I certainly didn't connect my stress and anxiety with my holiness compromises. I was a brand-new follower of Christ, and yet I wasn't satisfied with His love and the love of many wonderful new believing friends. I also wanted a boyfriend—someone to love me whether or not he was God's

best for me, and whether or not I compromised God's standards in the process.

I intentionally hid the nature of my relationship from my Christian friends, knowing they would press me toward holiness. I knew perfectly well that I was being disobedient, and I did it anyway. It took quite some time for me to realize that the fights with my boyfriend, my distance from God, the conflict with friends, and my unusual level of exhaustion and stress at work were all (directly or indirectly) ramifications of that choice. Ramifications allowed by a God who was using pain to wake me up.

Friends, we have to confront the reality that sometimes the problems in our lives do not come because "we're living in a broken world," or "the enemy is attacking us." Sometimes our problems are a direct result of us failing to exercise self-control. We are not living in obedience. Just as we, as loving parents, will not let our children compromise without consequences, neither will our loving heavenly Father. He is calling us back to a path that will bring peace.

Reflect

If you are honest with yourself, in what ways are you satisfying your own desires and not living up to God's standards of holiness? Pray now, repenting of your disobedience and asking God to help you change. Then commit to God and to a close friend that you will walk in holiness from now on.

Notes

_____

_____

_____

_____

_____

_____

_____

> "YOU EXPRESS LOVE
> BY OBEDIENCE."
>
> — Dr. Jack Hyles

In this world you will have trouble. But
take heart! I have overcome the world.
— John 16:33, NIV

Knowing the End
of the Story

Have you ever known someone who reads the last few pages of
a book before they start the beginning of the book? One friend
of mine reads the ending of every book first. It puts her mind
at ease to know how the story will end—whether it's happy or
sad and who lives or dies. This habit always seemed funny to
me, since knowing the ending takes all the tension out of the
intense chapters. At least I thought it was a funny habit, until I
was reading one particular book and literally begged a friend
to tell me what happened next. I needed reassurance that the
story would turn out right in the end.

Our lives are a story. As we scroll through, page by page, some
chapters are victorious, while others are full of struggle. Some
are a bit mundane, but others contain milestones such as
marriage, the birth of a child or grandchild, a big move, or a
new job. Some are scary: that day we got a diagnosis or a loved
one died.

Our stories are woven with many threads, including joy,
worry, struggle, happiness, and—since we can't know what will
happen tomorrow—the great unknown.

But what if we knew the ending? Would that change how we
read the suspenseful chapter that we're in right now? How
would we interpret those few pages that were filled with
sadness or struggle?

As Christ followers, we do know the ending of our story. Jesus Himself tells us the plot: we will have trouble in this world, but He has overcome the world! There will be chapters of pain and heartbreak because we live in a big, broken, messy world. But then He flips to the last chapter because He wants us to know that in the end, He will defeat everything that makes us sad, scared, or defeated. We can't see eternity yet, but we can cling to the truth that once and for all, God does win against the enemy. And as children of God, we win too.

What is worrying you today? What dark threads of fear are trying to weave their way into your story? Trouble may be there, but fear doesn't have to be. In intense times, remind yourself that you know the ultimate ending. For those who are followers of Jesus, He promises us that the last chapter of our story is well worth it.

Reflect

How does your view of the current chapter of your life change when you remember that Jesus told you to take heart because He has overcome the world?

Notes

_____

_____

_____

_____

_____

_____

_____

_____

"I'VE READ THE LAST PAGE
OF THE BIBLE. IT'S ALL GOING
TO TURN OUT ALL RIGHT."

— Billy Graham

You are the light of the world. . . . Let your light shine
before others, so that they may see your good works
and give glory to Your Father who is in heaven.
— Matthew 5:14-16, ESV

Shine Where You Are

While in a shop in Ireland, a friend was drawn to a beautiful silver cross. It looked as if it had been woven out of straw, with four arms tied at the end and a square in the middle. She learned that it was known as St. Brigid's Cross.

Back in the fifth century, a girl named Brigid went to visit a clan chief on his deathbed. He was incoherent and wildly inconsolable. Brigid probably felt a bit helpless to do much for him, so she settled in at his bedside simply to be there with him.

As she sat, Brigid gathered up a few of the rushes that covered the dirt floor in the room and began weaving a cross. The man watched her, and soon he quieted down enough to start asking questions about what she was doing. He asked what the cross of Christ signified. It is said that Brigid was able to explain the love of Jesus to the man, and he was baptized on his deathbed.

The cross wasn't fancy, and neither is the story. It involves a woman revealing Christ in the simple act of being where God called her and using the resources around her. She literally used what was under her feet to bring Jesus into the room!

We may sometimes feel like our daily work is uninspiring, monotonous, and unimportant to the Kingdom. We are "only" in the office, shuttling kids between activities, or taking an aging parent to doctor's appointments. It sure doesn't feel like

we're on the mission field. God's purpose in our lives seems like a goal in the very distant future, but certainly not right now. And that feeling can be so discouraging!

Yet that weariness goes away as we truly grasp this amazing, awesome, eternal truth: no matter the activity—big or small, fascinating or boring—God uses us where we are. We can be a testament to his goodness everywhere if we will only open our eyes and hearts to what He would have us do in each moment. Whether we are in the office with a frustrating coworker who needs a little kindness, with our kids in the car, or at the doctor's office for our parent's appointments, we can shine His light anywhere.

Go about your work today asking God to open your eyes to this truth, and to use you exactly where you are.

Reflect

How might you shine God's light in the little
things of life, exactly where you will be today?

Notes

_____

_____

_____

_____

_____

_____

_____

_____

"PEACE BEGINS
WITH A SMILE."

— Mother Teresa

I have learned to be content whatever the circumstances.
I know what it is to be in need, and I know what it is to
have plenty. I have learned the secret of being content
in any and every situation.
— *Philippians 4:11-12, NIV*

Choose Your Lens

Not long ago, I tried on a pair of jeans at a consignment store that didn't look so great in the shadowy dressing-room mirror. I was taking them back to the rack when I saw a newer mirror in the main room outside, and decided to take a quick second look. Score! The jeans looked completely different once I looked in a better mirror. The mirrors in the dressing room were older and darker, giving a distorted reflection that almost fooled me.

We've all looked at ourselves in distorted mirrors. What we may not realize, though, is that we often see everyday life—especially our challenging circumstances—through a similarly distorted lens. Oh, if only such-and-such was different, I'd feel better, is a common refrain. If only my husband realized what I have to deal with every day is another. The view through that lens makes us discontented and tempts us to grumble.

We try to change our discontentment by changing what we think has led to it. We try to amass more money to get out of that tiny apartment. We try to change how our kids appear to the outside world. We try to force our spouse to do things our way ("The right way!").

The result? Exhaustion. Leading right back to disappointment and discontent.

Shift Your Perspective

Or perhaps instead we just grumble a bit about the inconvenience or injustice of the situation. Once those emotions start taking root in our hearts, they often leak out onto our classmates, kids, spouse, coworkers, or friends.

The result? Yet again, exhaustion. Further discontent.

No matter what is going on, we can set aside our "right" to be discontented. Instead, we can take God's challenge to find contentment in every situation. Instead of looking through the lens that shows the most unflattering perspective, let's choose the one that changes everything.

That lens is called gratitude. Gratitude for everything God has allowed us to have that is good (that we might not be focusing on right now) and gratitude that He is sufficient. Not just sufficient to get us through what is difficult—and bear up both us and the scowl on our face—but sufficient to bring us through difficult times with a joyful heart!

Try practicing gratitude today. The facts of the situation won't change, but your perspective on them will. You may not be able to control your circumstances, but every day you do have control over how you view them.

Reflect

Every season of life has its challenges. What
can you be grateful for in the challenge that
you are going through right now? How can
you maintain that perspective over time?

Notes

_____

_____

_____

_____

_____

_____

_____

_____

"GRATITUDE IS NOT ONLY THE GREATEST OF VIRTUES, BUT THE PARENT OF ALL THE OTHERS."

— Marcus Tullius Cicero

Blessed are the poor in spirit, for
theirs is the kingdom of heaven.
— *Matthew 5:3, NIV*

Seeing Your Need for Him

My teenage daughter had been having a horrible, no good, very bad day. A bad month, really. Her best friends had fractured apart due to personality conflicts, and her closest friend had walked away from her entirely. My naturally shy daughter had finally found a place where she belonged—and now it was all gone.

I gave her lots of hugs and tried to draw her out. My heart hurt as I watched her pain; I longed to be there for her as a support. But day by day I saw her withdraw into herself. "No, I can't explain what's going on. I don't want to talk about it, Mom."

Maybe you know the feeling. Perhaps you are laboring under a load of sadness from a broken relationship, deep hurt, or other betrayal. Maybe you invested your time or energy into something only to have it all taken away. Maybe except for deep feelings of rejection, you are empty.

Take heart, because you are not alone. Someone is hurting right alongside you as He watches your pain. He is longing to hug you and make it better. He wants to be there for you as a support. He wants you to come to Him just as you are, before you have anything figured out. He loves you when you are broken, empty, with nothing to give.

Poor in spirit.

A month into my daughter's ordeal, I went in and prayed for her as usual before bedtime. Finally, after a few moments of inner struggle, she began to truly share, to trust me with her broken heart. And as we walked together before the throne of grace, she began to cast her cares on her heavenly Father and trust that He would heal.

When we set aside our pride, self-consciousness, and self-protectiveness to come before God in our deep need, it is as if we step into a parallel reality. We get a glimpse of the true reality all around us—the eternal reality called the Kingdom of Heaven—and realize that the One who wants to enfold us in His loving arms is also the One sitting on the throne. The sense of fulfillment is so profound that millions look in all the wrong places for it. Yet it is as close as admitting our need for and receiving the love of the One who will make all things new.

Reflect

Where you have brokenness, sadness, or emptiness, are
you holding back, or are you coming as you are before
God's throne? How will it bless you to come before Him?

Notes

_____

_____

_____

_____

_____

_____

_____

_____

"YOU DON'T REALLY
KNOW JESUS IS ALL
YOU NEED UNTIL JESUS
IS ALL YOU HAVE."

– Tim Keller
*Walking With God Through
Pain and Suffering.*

*For he has rescued us from the kingdom of darkness
and transferred us into the Kingdom of his dear Son.*
— *Colossians 1:13*

Underground
Espionage Agents

There is a mental shift that will change everything about how we view our lives. We need to realize who we really are. I don't just mean embracing our identity in Christ or the fact that we are daughters of the King. I mean recognizing something much bigger: We are key players in a great war between the Kingdom of God and the kingdom of darkness, and this earth is the primary battlefield.

The anxieties that take our time, create stress, and divert our attention fade into insignificance once we have that perspective. Other things become far, far more important. And suddenly we realize we have a calling beyond ourselves.

The Bible says Satan is "god of this world," (2 Corinthians 4:4), "the commander of the powers in the unseen world" (Ephesians 2:2) and "the ruler of this world" (John 12:31). That doesn't mean that Satan is in ultimate control—our God still reigns over everything—but it does mean that we are living in occupied territory. Once humanity chose sin, the evil one was given the power to rule over this broken world, tempt its people, and spread misunderstanding, division, natural and physical disasters, and spiritual destruction.

And yet, Jesus says that there is another Kingdom! (John 18:36). Once we commit our lives to Christ, we cease being

citizens of earth and become citizens of heaven. From that point on, we are called to actively undermine the kingdom in which we are living, on behalf of another King. In other words, we are underground espionage agents. Like the French Underground in World War II, we are called to rescue the captives bound for destruction, to be agents of light in a kingdom of darkness.

Our primary job on this earth is not any of the many hats we wear (wife, girlfriend, mom, grandma, saleswoman, neighbor ...). Our primary job is to be an agent of Almighty God; to care for people in need; to show kindness when all others would be provoked; to share the Good News through our words and lives; to love one another in a world marked by the evil one's division.

Once we live from this eternal perspective, suddenly we will know which worries, time-wasting distractions, and irritations simply don't matter. We will realize that no matter how much God loves us, this life is not about us. He is calling us to be part of a much bigger story.

Reflect

In which areas have you been distracted
by worries and stress in recent days and
weeks? How do those worries change if
you adopt an eternal perspective? In what
one or two areas is God calling you to make
an eternal difference for His Kingdom?

Notes

"ONE OF THE GREAT BENEFITS OF
OUR 'ERA OF OPPORTUNITY'
IS THAT ONCE WE HAVE THAT
VISION AND THAT WAY TO
MAKE THE RIGHT DECISIONS
ON THOSE OPPORTUNITIES,
THE STAGE IS SET FOR US AS
WOMEN TO MAKE AN ETERNAL
DIFFERENCE IN THIS WORLD."

— Shaunti Feldhahn
The Life Ready Woman:
Thriving in a Do-It-All World

This is the day which the Lord has made;
Let us rejoice and be glad in it.
— Psalm 118:24, NASB

Savor Each Day

Every fan of science fiction knows that at warp speed, everything flows by in a blur. And just like any starship worth mentioning, we busy women often rush from point A to point B, from task to task, without taking in the journey in between.

God tells us that one antidote to feeling pressed in on every side is to stop and notice each day and what He is doing with it. After all, we can't "be glad" for God's great works unless we purposefully take in the day that is flowing by.

This reminds me of a great regret of mine that turned into a great lesson. After months of planning our wedding, the actual ceremony seemed to pass in a delightful blur. A few weeks later, my husband mentioned seeing a particular couple who had been at the ceremony but had to miss the reception. I said, "Really? I don't remember seeing them. It all seemed to go so fast—I don't remember much about the ceremony itself."

Jeff smiled sideways. "I remember everything." He then told me that one of his groomsmen, a man who was already married, had taken him aside ahead of time and told him the day could either rush by or be soaked in. "He encouraged me to purposefully enter into it and remember it all. So I made sure to really enjoy every moment."

I was glad for him, but regretful for me. In some ways, I had missed my own wedding.

Shift Your Perspective

Years later, when our kids were born, I heard echoes of that advice from older moms who said, "Oh, enjoy this time. It goes so quickly." This time, I decided, I would not let the warp speed of life turn these precious years into a blur. I have tried to savor and soak in every moment, every stage.

It has been so rewarding. Unlike my wedding ceremony, I have thousands of rich, delightful memories with my kids that will still be precious long after they leave home.

Whether it is about time with family, friends, career, or the use of a particular gift, letting the days slip by and wondering "where did the time go?" is a surefire way to end up with weariness and regret. Let's instead resolve to notice each day, and be glad in it.

Reflect

Are you rejoicing and savoring each day, or is your life one big blur? How can you focus on each moment?

Notes

_____

_____

_____

_____

_____

_____

_____

_____

"WHEN YOU ARISE IN THE MORNING, THINK OF WHAT A PRECIOUS PRIVILEGE IT IS TO BE ALIVE – TO BREATHE, TO THINK, TO ENJOY, TO LOVE."

— Marcus Aurelius

Be honest in your evaluation of yourselves, measuring
yourselves by the faith God has given us. Just as our
bodies have many parts and each part has a special
function, so it is with Christ's body. We are many parts
of one body, and we all belong to each other.
— Romans 12:3-5

The Right Yoke: Embracing Who You Are NOT

We're often told to be who we are. This also means cheerfully embracing who we are *not*. Much of our weariness stems from continuously trying to force a square peg into a round hole.

For several years, that was me. I am a social researcher, and I speak at a lot of women's retreats, conferences, and marriage seminars. I love seeing the light bulb go on and watching relationship transformation. But for a while I dreaded these events because of the many hurting men and women who came afterward for serious counsel. They would share heart-wrenching stories of a spouse's betrayal or a child's addiction and ask for specific advice.

I felt like I should be able to help with their individual hurts and trials—I mean, what kind of a relationship author was I otherwise?—so I would listen, try to give advice, and share things from my research that applied. But I arrived home totally wiped out.

Finally, I realized: I'm not a counselor. I'm a teacher, encourager, researcher, eye-opener . . . but not a therapist. So instead of feeling like there was something wrong with me as a relationship author, I started to tell the event organizers, "I'm not a counselor; is there someone I can refer difficult situations to?" And the weight miraculously lifted. I began to listen to the hurting person without pressure, cry with them, pray for them—and refer them to a real counselor.

How has God *not* wired you? Embrace it. Are you an introvert who feels that you "should" like the dinner parties your husband loves to throw? If you two keep fighting over this, embrace the fact that God has wired you to not be an extrovert and that you need recharging with a one-on-one conversation or a good book.

Yes, we need to push ourselves out of our comfort zones to fulfill callings that God asks of us, like hospitality to others and service to our spouse. But God also asks us to see ourselves with sober judgment. So perhaps you can compromise with your husband on the number of get-togethers a month or explain that the day after game night you need downtime. Perhaps you can learn to focus on one-on-one conversation with the friend next to you at the dinner table instead of entering into the buzz of ten other people.

Celebrating who we are—and are not—is the key to fitting joyfully into our place in the body of Christ.

Reflect

Is there something you've been trying to do or be that is not who you are? If it is important for your marriage or life in some way, how can you both embrace who you are not and achieve the necessary goals?

Notes

_____

_____

_____

_____

_____

_____

_____

"IT'S AT THE HEART OF EVERYTHING WE STRUGGLE WITH IN LIFE: LONGING TO BE VALUABLE, TO BE ACCEPTED, TO BE PRIZED, TO BE WORTH SOMETHING TO SOMEBODY, TO HAVE A LIFE THAT MATTERS, AND GOD'S SAYING 'YOU MATTER! I DIDN'T MAKE ANYONE ELSE LIKE YOU. YOU'RE NOT A REPRINT OR A LITHOGRAPH. YOU'RE A ONE-OF-A-KIND, ORIGINAL CREATION OF GOD.'"

— Louie Giglio

Moses' arms soon became so tired he could no longer
hold them up. So Aaron and Hur found a stone for him
to sit on. Then they stood on each side of Moses, holding
up his hands. So his hands held steady until sunset.
— *Exodus 17:12*

Let Someone Hold
Up Your Arms

It gets me every time—my eyes well up as I watch the video
of Olympic sprinter Derek Redmond, who massively injured
his hamstring midway through his race in the 1992 Barcelona
games. He started hopping toward the finish line, his pain
palpable as he boldly tried to finish the race, even though he
had no hope of winning a medal. Even more touching is what
Redmond's father did next. Jim Redmond leapt out of the
stands and shook off security guards as he ran to help his son
reach his goal. The picture of a father holding up his son as
he wept in pain and disappointment makes it one of the most
inspiring moments in Olympic history. It's such a clear visual
of the raw, messy, beautiful lengths to which we go to serve and
love someone we care about.

We like to identify with the father in that story because we can
probably imagine doing something similar for someone we
love. But if we're honest, there are times in our busy, stressful
lives when we are more like the injured runner. It sometimes
seems as if we cannot take one more step forward without
falling on our face. Whether it's a troubled relationship, a
bad diagnosis, our child's behavioral issues at school, job
insecurity . . . it all weighs heavy on us, and sometimes it feels
like we can't go on.

Create Life-Giving Relationships

Of course, we women like to limp along and pretend we can handle it on our own. We actually do a banner job of it. But you know what? There are people in our lives who want to leap the railing, run to our side, and grab hold of us as we try to reach the finish line. People who would consider it an honor to walk alongside us and be our companions during the difficult parts of our race.

We need to let them grab our arms and help.

Yes, it means being vulnerable. It means the secret will be out that we cannot handle everything on our own. It feels risky, even embarrassing, to ask for help. But the beauty of allowing someone to help us as we limp toward the finish line brings tears to the eyes—a display of love (both in the giving and the receiving) that reminds us that we are never, ever alone.

Reflect

Have you ever come alongside someone as they struggled? Think about how honored you felt to help them. Now think about someone who has offered to help you. Pray for God's help to set aside your pride and allow them to take hold of your arms and help you across the finish line today.

Notes

_____

_____

_____

_____

_____

_____

_____

"NO ACT OF KINDNESS,
NO MATTER HOW SMALL,
IS EVER WASTED."

— Aesop

A wife of noble character who can find? She is worth far more than rubies. Her husband has full confidence in her and lacks nothing of value. She brings him good, not harm, all the days of her life.
— *Proverbs 31:10-12, NIV*

The Big, Pretty Picture

When I read about the Proverbs 31 woman, I'm both inspired and overwhelmed by her example. She made food, bought fields, generated profits, bought a vineyard, traded, stayed up late, got up early, clothed her family, stylishly dressed herself, and was a dynamite teacher—all with a whole lot of wisdom. She served the poor, ran her household, was never lazy, and her children adored her. Her husband and community constantly praised her.

Most days I wish I could check just one of those boxes, and I would consider it a big win! It is very easy to feel inferior with this snapshot of womanhood taped to my mirror, calling me to look like this someday.

But the Proverbs 31 woman is not a real woman! This is not Mary or Elizabeth or Rachel. This is not a portrait of an actual woman at some ultimate moment in time when she "has it all together."

Proverbs 31 is a big-picture view of the life of a woman of noble character—not a description of someone who does all these things perfectly, all at once.

This description of a woman of noble character shows us what God values and gives us something to aspire to. But He also gives us seasons. As newborns grow into toddlers, then adolescents, then young adults, our responsibilities as parents

change too. The same applies to our lives as women of faith. There are seasons of young children and there are seasons of empty nesting. There are seasons of community involvement or business, and there are seasons of keeping our heads down and focusing on our family and marriage. There are seasons when we have margin to buy that field and the fixer-upper house on it, and completely different seasons when we can take the time to seek out from afar and cook the perfect paleo/organic/no-red-dye food for our family.

We must not feel bad for devoting ourselves to the season God has called us into.

Are there things we'd like to do once we have more time? Of course! Do we have ministry goals or work aspirations for when the time is right? Absolutely. But let's commit to praying for wisdom to know what God is calling us to do right now to bring Him glory in our particular season. Being obedient to that call will be what paints a beautiful, big picture of a life that points directly to Him.

Reflect

Where do you sense God is calling you to focus in this particular season? What might you be called to set aside, in order to bring Him glory in what you are doing?

Notes

_____

_____

_____

_____

_____

_____

_____

_____

"YOU CAN'T HAVE AN EXCITING, SUCCESSFUL, POWERFUL CAREER AND AT THE SAME TIME WIN THE MOTHER-OF-THE-YEAR AWARD AND BE WIFE AND LOVER EXTRAORDINAIRE. NO ONE CAN. IF YOU SEE SUCCESSFUL, GLAMOROUS WOMEN ON MAGAZINE COVERS PROCLAIMING THEY DO IT ALL, BELIEVE ME, YOU'RE NOT GETTING THE WHOLE STORY."

— Maria Shriver,
*Ten Things I Wish I'd Known –
Before I Went Out Into the Real World*

Submit yourselves therefore to God. Resist the devil, and he will flee from you. Draw near to God, and he will draw near to you.
— *James 4:7-8, ESV*

Resist and Draw Near

A friend began to really enjoy her subscriptions to beautiful fashion magazines. Yet she realized it was taking an unexpected toll. She began shopping more, spending far beyond her budget, and became envious of others. Even among women in her Bible study she found herself coveting that necklace, those shoes, that car. It wasn't long before her appetite for the newest clothes and jewelry took a toll beyond the discontent in her heart. Her marriage was in trouble.

Satan knows exactly how to tempt us. And he has come to steal, kill, and destroy. He plots how to pull us away from God. He experiments: which temptation will we follow to our destruction? It may start small—a growing dissatisfaction with our lives as we scroll through social media, compare marital war stories with friends, or look enviously at those who are married while we're still single. Maybe it is the negative chatter in our heads that we are unworthy to be loved, don't deserve that promotion at work, or aren't good at Pinterest-worthy home decorating. Or it could be something big, like debilitating health issues.

Scripture gives a clear two-part solution: immediately resist the devil, and draw near to our heavenly Father. We must stop supporting what the evil one is doing. Maybe it means deleting a social media app or taping Scripture on your mirror to remind you of God's love for you. Maybe it means committing to resist the sneaky pleasure of complaining about your husband to

your girlfriends, and instead saying only positive and loving things to and about him.

Scripture says that if we resist the devil, he will flee. The only way to do that is to draw close to God. He longs for us to have a thriving, close friendship with Him, marked by time in the Bible, prayer, listening, worship, and gratitude for our blessings. When we come near to God, He promises to come near to us.

When my fashion-crazy friend realized what was happening, she knew she had to stop the ugliness growing inside her. She took the hard step of canceling all her fashion magazine subscriptions. She realized she even had to stop looking at those magazines at the gym and the grocery checkout lane. And as she prayed, God immediately helped her notice and be grateful for the many blessings she already had. Which, she realized, was a much more enjoyable way to live.

Reflect

What is one area where the enemy has probably been trying to tempt you to destruction? What one thing can you start doing today to resist him? What can you do that will draw you nearer to God?

Notes

_____

_____

_____

_____

_____

_____

_____

_____

"GOOD JUDGMENT COMES FROM EXPERIENCE. AND A LOT OF THAT COMES FROM BAD JUDGMENT."

— Will Rogers

Let us therefore come boldly to the throne of grace, that we
may obtain mercy and find grace to help in time of need.
— *Hebrews 4:16, NKJV*

Run to the Throne

There is a scene in the movie *Anna and the King* that always chokes me up. A young girl rushes through a massive set of doors into the throne room of a mighty king. Hundreds of supplicants are bowing in reverence (and some in fear) before his throne. Interrupting everything, ignoring every bit of protocol, she rushes past all the people and jumps into the arms of the king. Everyone is shocked . . . but they shouldn't be, because this mighty king is her father. He picks her up, sets aside all the business of the throne room, and carries her out the door to attend to something that is far more important—her.

Sisters, we have a heavenly Father who gives us that same access to Him! He is the King of Kings and the Creator of the universe. He holds the unimaginable depths of the universe together with a word of His power. And yet He tells us we can "come boldly to the throne of grace." What an amazing privilege!

I think we often forget that we are beloved daughters of God. He adores us and longs for us to come to Him and boldly ask Him for help. I remember that feeling as a mom of young toddlers. When my daughter or son fell down at the park and skinned a knee, there was a moment where they would search until they made eye contact with me. And then they would run to me. When that happened, my heart knew that they trusted me. They knew they were loved. They knew I would kiss them, comfort them, and do whatever I could to help them. I can't

help but think that our heavenly Father feels pleased when we do the same with Him.

We so often feel battered and bruised in places that a Band-Aid won't cover. Our hearts feel hurt by relationships that disappoint us. Our minds struggle to keep anxiety at bay. Our bodies feel tired and pulled in a hundred different directions. It requires a certain amount of confidence and vulnerability to trust that if we run boldly to God's throne, He will respond with open arms.

Dare to trust your Father with your heart. You will find grace in your time of need.

Reflect

Close your eyes and imagine yourself running through the doors and into the courts of your heavenly Father. What do you want to approach His throne of grace with today? Write down your prayer, and note anything you think He wants you to trust Him with.

Notes

_____

_____

_____

_____

_____

_____

_____

"FAITH IS TO BELIEVE WHAT YOU DO NOT SEE; THE REWARD OF THIS FAITH IS TO SEE WHAT YOU BELIEVE."

— Saint Augustine

*I tell you the truth, the Son can do nothing by
himself. He does only what he sees the Father
doing. Whatever the Father does, the Son also does.*
— John 5:19

Do Only What You See
Your Father Doing

It had been one of those days. I faced a to-do list mountain, conference calls that went way too long, missed deadlines, and urgent messages from every direction—and I didn't handle it well. After apologizing for the fifth time for snapping at my kids and my husband, I tucked the kids into bed and curled up with a book.

But I quickly sensed that gentle whisper from Holy Spirit, calling me to stop what I was doing and listen. I tried, but my thoughts and worries kept swirling. So I decided to pick just one thing on my to-do list and pray about it; a thorny decision about a particular initiative for my ministry. As soon as my thoughts focused on this worry, the Lord's whisper became so clear: "Is that initiative even what I've called you to focus on right now?"

Honest answer? No, it wasn't. All the things on my to-do list seemed important, but in fact were distracting me from what I knew had to be my two main professional callings for that season: writing my next book and speaking to the groups that had invited me. Worse, they were distracting me from my first calling as a wife and mom.

Live According to Your Design

How can we stop ourselves from ending up with all these "important" things that God hasn't asked us to do? In his landmark study, *Experiencing God*, Henry Blackaby reminds us that rather than picking good things to do and asking God to bless them, we need to look to see where God is working, and go join Him.

Two thousand years ago, Jesus walked around the pool of Bethesda—an area filled with the hurting, sick, and injured. He spoke to and healed just one man. A short time later, He explained why He bypassed the "multitude" at the pool to focus on the one: "I can do nothing by myself. I do only what I see my Father doing. Whatever my Father does, I do." Which also means, by definition, "I do not do those things that my Father isn't doing and leading me to do."

If Jesus was willing to pass up the multitude and trust in His Father's plan, we need to be able to pass up multitudes of opportunities—good things!—in the same way. That will allow us to do the one thing God is doing.

Reflect

What are some seemingly good things in your life that God may not be doing, and which are getting in the way of the better things that He has called you to do?

Notes

_____

_____

_____

_____

_____

_____

_____

_____

"WHENEVER YOU SAY YES TO SOMETHING, THERE IS LESS OF YOU FOR SOMETHING ELSE. MAKE SURE YOUR YES IS WORTH THE LESS."

— Lysa TerKeurst,
*The Best Yes: Making Wise Decisions
in the Midst of Endless Demands*

And this is my prayer: that your love may abound
more and more in knowledge and depth of insight,
so that you may be able to discern what is best and
may be pure and blameless for the day of Christ.
— *Philippians 1:9-10, NIV*

It HAS to Be Finished?

Do you ever think you're a bit obsessive about having to finish a particular task you're engrossed in? Most of us have that quirk, and its results cause us a lot of unnecessary regret.

Laurie came to this realization when her kids reached high school. She decided to have a garage sale to sell off all the good-condition grade-school stuff—and have an excuse to trash the stained clothes, smelly roller blades, and partial Playmobil sets.

Soon, though, her goal expanded to include the two walk-in attic storage areas. She describes it this way: "An intoxicating power of minimalism came over me! What a great opportunity to get rid of everything we didn't currently use in case we decided to finish off the largest space into a guest bedroom." Obsessed with getting rid of 25 years of clutter, the simple project mushroomed into a two-headed behemoth.

After several consecutive weeks of preparing for the now-monster garage sale, my friend finally realized that her family was eating only pizzas and McDonald's, and bumming rides to activities. And there may have been a few times that her telephone voice was a tad sweeter to the sales reps than to her family when they interrupted her Great Purge of the Century. Sound familiar?

My friend asked God for help to break the "It HAS to be FINISHED" cycle. He gave her an idea to help her pay attention to what's really important. She calls it SLOW: **Surrender, Listen, Obey, Walk Away.**

First, I Surrender the "It HAS to be DONE" list to my greater call. Can this activity be done later? Does it really have to be done at all? Listen to that quiet, still Voice inside. If my priorities are wrong, He will tell me. Will I listen? Then Obey. If taking my elderly mother out for coffee is truly the "what is best" thing for now, I need to ask God to help me overcome my compelling drive to finish the task. Then quickly Walk Away from the task before getting sucked back into it. If necessary, I can delegate the task, or perhaps reschedule the completion for another time.

When we are driven by our "It HAS to be done" compulsion, we run over those most in our way—and we often have regrets. By taking it SLOW, we know we gave our best energy and time to the people and projects that truly matter most.

Reflect

When in the past have you been so compelled
to finish something that you ran over a more
important priority? What are you working on
now that might need a SLOW approach?

Notes

_____

_____

_____

_____

_____

_____

_____

_____

"WISELY, AND SLOW. THEY STUMBLE THAT RUN FAST."

— William Shakespeare